CROCHET

Wildflower Hot Pads & Towel Toppers™

Designs by Patricia Hall

General Information

Many of th......ed in this pattern book can be purchased from local craft, fabric and variety stores, or from the Annie's Att......Catalog *(see Customer Service information on page 15).*

Contents

General Instructions

These decorative Hot Pads and Towel Toppers are made with acrylic yarn, which may melt when exposed to extreme heat. You may wish to substitute cotton worsted yarn if you plan to use the items for removing hot items from the oven or for protecting surfaces from very hot dishes. Always use extreme care when using any hand-crocheted item while cooking since open spaces between stitches could allow burns and uneven surfaces could cause spills.

Marigold

SKILL LEVEL

EASY

FINISHED SIZES

Hot Pad: 10½ inches across
Towel Topper: 9½ inches across

MATERIALS

❑ Red Heart Classic medium (worsted) weight yarn (3½ oz/190 yds/ 99g per skein):
    1 skein each #289 copper and #686 paddy green
❑ Red Heart Fine fine (fine) weight yarn (2½ oz/ 240 yds/ 70g per skein):
    1 skein each #254 pumpkin and #687 paddy green
❑ Sizes H/8/5mm, I/9/5.5mm, J/10/6mm and K/10½/6.5mm crochet hooks or sizes needed to obtain gauge
❑ Sewing needle
❑ Kitchen towel
❑ Matching sewing thread

GAUGE

Size H hook and 1 strand fine weight yarn: 2 dc rows = 1 inch
Size I hook and 1 strand medium weight yarn: 2 dc rows = 1¼ inches
Size J hook and 2 strands fine weight yarn: Rnds 1 and 2 of Front = 1½ inches across
Size K hook and 2 strands medium weight yarn: Rnds 1 and 2 of Front = 2¼ inches across

PATTERN NOTE

Join with a slip stitch unless otherwise stated.

SPECIAL STITCH

Triple treble crochet (trtr): Yo 4 times, insert hook in next st, yo, pull lp through, [yo, pull through 2 lps on hook] 5 times.

INSTRUCTIONS

HOT PAD

FRONT

Rnd 1: With size K hook and 2 strands copper held tog as 1, ch 4, join in beg ch to form ring, ch 1, 8 sc in ring, join in beg sc. *(8 sc)*

Rnds 2 & 3: Working these rnds i back lps *(see Stitch Guide)*, ch 1, sc in each st around, join in beg s *(16 sc, 32 sc)*

Rnd 4: Working this rnd in back lp ch 1, 2 sc in first st, sc in each of ne 3 sts, [2 sc in next st, sc in each next 3 sts] around, join in beg s Fasten off. *(40 sc)*

Rnd 5: With size K hook and 2 stran copper held tog as 1, working in re **front lps** *(see Stitch Guide)* of sts rnd 1, join in any st, (ch 3, dc, ch sl st) in same st, (sl st, ch 3, dc, ch 3, sl st) in each st around, join in beg sl st. Fasten off. *(40 petals)*

Rnds 6–8: Working in front lps of rnds 2–4, rep rnd 5.

BACK

Rnd 1: With size I hook and 1 strand copper, ch 4, join in beg ch to form ring, ch 3 *(counts as first dc)*, 15 dc in ring, join in 3rd ch of beg ch-3. *(16 dc)*

Rnd 2: (Ch 3, dc) in first st, 2 dc in each st around, join in 3rd ch of beg ch-3. *(32 dc)*

Rnd 3: Ch 3, dc in each of next 2 sts, 2 dc in next st, [dc in each of next 3 sts, 2 dc in next st] around, join in 3rd ch of beg ch-3. *(40 dc)*

Rnd 4: Holding Front and Back WS tog with Back facing, matching sts, working through both thicknesses, ch 1, 2 sc in each st around, join in beg sc. Fasten off. *(80 sc)*

Rnd 5: With RS facing and size I hook and 2 strands medium weight paddy green held tog as 1, join with sc in first st, *ch 2, tr in next st, **dtr** *(see Stitch Guide)* in next st, **trtr** *(see Special Stitch)* in each of next 2 sts, dtr in next st, tr in next st, ch 2**, sc in each of next 2 sts, rep from* around, ending last rep at**, sc in last st, join in beg sc. *(80 sts)*

Rnd 6: *Sl st in each of next 2 chs, sl st next st, sc in next st, 2 sc in next st, ch 3, sc in 2nd ch from hook, sc in next ch, 2 sc in next st, sc in next st, sl st next st, sl st in each of next

2 chs**, sl st in each of next 2 sts, rep from * around, ending last rep at **, sl st in last st, join in joining sl st of last rnd. Fasten off.

TOWEL TOPPER
FRONT

Rnd 1: With size J hook and 2 strands pumpkin held tog as 1, ch 4, join in beg ch to form ring, ch 1, 8 sc in ring, join in beg sc. *(8 sc)*

Rnds 2 & 3: Working these rnds in **back lps** *(see Stitch Guide)*, ch 1, 2 sc in each st around, join in beg sc. *(16 sc, 32 sc)*

Rnd 4: Working this rnd in back lps, ch 1, 2 sc in first st, sc in each of next 3 sts, [2 sc in next st, sc in each of next 3 sts] around, join in beg sc. Fasten off. *(40 sc)*

Rnd 5: With size J hook and 2 strands pumpkin held tog as 1, working in rem **front lps** *(see Stitch Guide)* of sts on rnd 1, join in any st, (ch 3, dc, ch 3, sl st) in same st, (sl st, ch 3, dc, ch 3, sl st) in each st around, join in beg sl st. Fasten off. *(40 petals)*

Rnds 6–8: Working in front lps of rnds 2–4, rep rnd 5.

BACK

Rnd 1: With size H hook and 1 strand pumpkin, ch 4, join in beg ch to form ring, ch 3 *(counts as first dc)*, 15 dc in ring, join in 3rd ch of beg ch-3. *(16 dc)*

Rnd 2: (Ch 3, dc) in first st, 2 dc in each st around, join in 3rd ch of beg ch-3. *(32 dc)*

Rnd 3: Ch 3, dc in each of next 2 sts, 2 dc in next st, [dc in each of next 3 sts, 2 dc in next st] around, join in 3rd ch of beg ch-3. *(40 dc)*

Rnd 4: Holding Front and Back WS tog with Back facing, matching sts, working through both thicknesses, ch 1, 2 sc in each st around, join in beg sc. Fasten off. *(80 sc)*

Rnd 5: With RS facing and size I hook and 2 strands fine weight paddy green held tog as 1, join with sc in first st, *ch 2, tr in next st, **dtr** *(see Stitch Guide)* in next st, **trtr** *(see Special Stitch)* in each of next 2 sts, dtr in next st, tr in next st, ch 2**, sc in each of next 2 sts, rep from* around, ending last rep at**, sc in last st, join in beg sc. *(80 sts)*

Rnd 6: *Sl st in each of next 2 chs, sl st next st, sc in next st, 2 sc in next st, ch 3, sc in 2nd ch from hook, sc in next ch, 2 sc in next st, sc in next st, sl st next st, sl st in each of next 2 chs**, sl st in each of next 2 sts, rep from * around, ending last rep at **, sl st in last st, join in joining sl st of last rnd. Fasten off.

FINISHING

1. Fold kitchen towel crosswise. With sewing needle and thread, st across fold; gather to fit across Back of Towel Topper and sew in place.

2. For **hanging lp**, with size H hook and fine weight paddy green, join in st on last rnd at center top, ch 12, sl st in same st. Fasten off. ❏❏

Daisy

SKILL LEVEL

EASY

FINISHED SIZES

Hot Pad: 11½ inches across
Towel Topper: 10½ inches across

MATERIALS

❏ Red Heart Classic medium (worsted) weight yarn (3½ oz/ 190 yds/99g per skein):
   1 skein each #1 white, #686 paddy green and #230 yellow
❏ Red Heart Fine fine (fine) weight yarn (2½ oz/240 yds/70g per skein):
   1 skein each #1 white, #687 paddy green and #230 yellow
❏ Sizes H/8/5mm, I/9/5.5mm, J/10/6mm and K/10½/6.5mm crochet hooks or sizes needed to obtain gauge
❏ Sewing needle
❏ Kitchen towel
❏ Matching sewing thread
❏ Stitch marker

GAUGE

Size H hook and 1 strand fine weight yarn: 2 dc rows = 1 inch
Size I hook and 1 strand medium weight yarn: 2 dc rows =1¼ inches
Size J hook and 2 strands fine weight yarn: 7 sts = 2 inches
Size K hook and 2 strands medium weight yarn: 3 sts = 1 inch

PATTERN NOTES

Join with a slip stitch unless otherwise stated.

Do not join or turn rounds unless otherwise stated. Mark first stitch of each round.

INSTRUCTIONS

HOT PAD
FRONT

Rnd 1: With size I hook and 2 strands medium weight yellow held tog as 1, ch 2, 6 sc in 2nd ch from hook. *(6 sc)*

Note: Work rnds 2–5 in **back lps** *(see Stitch Guide).*

Rnds 2 & 3: 2 sc in each st around. *(12 sc, 24 sc)*

Rnd 4: Sc in each st around.

Rnd 5: [Sc in next st, 2 sc in next st] around, join in beg sc. Fasten off. *(36 sc)*

Rnd 6: Working in both lps, with size K hook and 2 strands medium weight white held tog as 1, join in 2nd st, *ch 9, sc in 2nd ch from hook, sc in each of next 2 chs, hdc in each of last 5 chs, sk next 2 sts on rnd 5**, sl st in next st, rep from * around, ending last rep at **, join in beg sl st. Fasten off. *(12 petals)*

Rnd 7: With size K hook and 2 strands medium weight white held tog as 1, working behind petals in sk sts of rnd 5, join in first sk st, *ch 9, sc in 2nd ch from hook, sc in each of next 2 chs, hdc in each of last 5 chs, sk next sk st on rnd 5**, sl st in next st, rep from * around, ending last rep at **, join in beg sl st. Fasten off. *(12 petals)*

Rnd 8: With size K hook and 1 strand medium weight white, working behind petals in rem sk sts on rnd 5, join in any sk st, ch 4, [sl st in next sk st, ch 4] around, join in beg sl st. Fasten off. *(12 ch sps)*

Rnd 9: With size I hook and 2 strands medium weight yellow held tog as 1, working in rem **front lps** *(see Stitch Guide)* of rnds 1–4, join with sc in first st of rnd 1, [ch 3, sc in next st] around to last st of rnd 4. Fasten off.

BACK

Rnd 1: With size I hook and 1 strand medium weight white, ch 4, join in beg ch to form ring, ch 3 *(counts as first dc)*, 15 dc in ring, join in 3rd ch of beg ch-3. *(16 dc)*

Rnd 2: (Ch 3, dc) in first st, 2 dc in each st around, join in 3rd ch of beg ch-3. *(32 dc)*

Rnd 3: Ch 2 *(counts as first hdc)*, 2 hdc in next st, [hdc in next st, 2 hdc in next st] around, join in 2nd ch of beg ch-2. *(48 hdc)*

Rnd 4: Holding Front and Back WS tog with Back facing, working in ch-4 sps on rnd 8 of Front and sts on Back at same time, ch 1, 2 sc in first st on Back and first ch-4 sp on Front, sc in each of next 3 sts [2 sc in next st on Back and in next ch-4 sp on Front at same time, 3 sc in each of next 3 sts] around, join in beg sc. Fasten off. *(60 sc)*

Rnd 5: With RS facing and size I hook and 2 strands medium weight paddy green held tog as 1, join with sc in first st, sc in each st around, join in beg sc.

Rnd 6: *Ch 10, sc in 2nd ch from hook, sc in next ch, hdc in next ch, dc in next ch, tr in each of last 5 chs, sk next 4 sts on rnd 5**, sl st in next st, rep from * around, ending last rep at **, join in joining sl st of last rnd. Fasten off.

TOWEL TOPPER
FRONT

Rnd 1: With size H hook and 2 strands fine weight yellow held tog as 1, ch 2, 6 sc in 2nd ch from hook. *(6 sc)*

Note: Work rnds 2–5 in **back lps** *(see Stitch Guide).*

Rnds 2 & 3: 2 sc in each st around. *(12 sc, 24 sc)*

Rnd 4: Sc in each st around.

Rnd 5: [Sc in next st, 2 sc in next st] around, join in beg sc. Fasten off. *(36 sc)*

Rnd 6: Working in both lps, with size J hook and 2 strands fine weight white held tog as 1, join in 2nd st, *ch 9, sc in 2nd ch from hook, sc in each of next 2 chs, hdc in each of last 5 chs, sk next 2 sts on rnd 5**, sl st in next st, rep from * around, ending last rep at **, join in beg sl st. Fasten off. *(12 petals)*

Rnd 7: With size J hook and 2 strands fine weight white held tog as 1, working behind petals in sk sts of rnd 5, join in first sk st, for **petal**, *ch 9, sc in 2nd ch from hook, sc in each of next 2 chs, hdc in each of last 5 chs, sk next sk st on rnd 5**

sl st in next st, rep from * around, ending last rep at **, join in beg sl st. Fasten off. *(12 petals)*

Rnd 8: With size J hook and 1 strand fine weight white, working behind petals in rem sk sts on rnd 5, join in any sk st, ch 4, [sl st in next sk st, ch 4] around, join in beg sl st. Fasten off. *(12 ch sps)*

Rnd 9: With size H hook and 2 strands fine weight yellow held tog as 1, working in rem **front lps** *(Stitch Guide)* of rnds 1–4, join with sc in first st of rnd 1, [ch 3, sc in next st] around to last st of rnd 4. Fasten off.

BACK

Rnd 1: With size H hook and 1 strand fine weight white, ch 4, join in beg ch to form ring, ch 3 *(counts as first dc)*, 15 dc in ring, join in 3rd ch of beg ch-3. *(16 dc)*

Rnd 2: (Ch 3, dc) in first st, 2 dc in each st around, join in 3rd ch of beg ch-3. *(32 dc)*

Rnd 3: Ch 2 *(counts as first hdc)*, 2 hdc in next st, [hdc in next st, 2 hdc in next st] around, join in 2nd ch of beg ch-2. *(48 hdc)*

Rnd 4: Holding Front and Back WS tog with Back facing, working in ch-4 sps on rnd 8 of Front and sts on Back at same time, ch 1, 2 sc in first st on Back and first ch-4 sp on Front, sc in each of next 3 sts [2 sc in next st on Back and in next ch-4 sp on Front at same time, 3 sc in each of next 3 sts] around, join in beg sc. Fasten off. *(60 sc)*

Rnd 5: With RS facing and size H hook and 2 strands fine weight paddy green

held tog as 1, join with sc in first st, sc in each st around, join in beg sc.

Rnd 6: *Ch 10, sc in 2nd ch from hook, sc in next ch, hdc in next ch, dc in next ch, tr in each of last 5 chs, sk next 4 sts on rnd 5**, sl st in next st, rep from * around, ending last rep at **, join in joining sl st of last rnd. Fasten off.

FINISHING

1. Fold kitchen towel crosswise. With sewing needle and thread, st across fold; gather to fit across Back of Towel Topper and sew in place.

2. For **hanging lp**, with size H hook and fine weight paddy green, join in st on last rnd at center top, ch 12, sl st in same st. Fasten off. ❏❏

Peony

SKILL LEVEL

EASY

FINISHED SIZES

Hot Pad: 10½ inches across
Towel Topper: 9½ inches across

MATERIALS

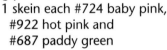

- ❑ Red Heart Classic medium (worsted) weight yarn (3½ oz/190 yds/ 99g per skein): **4 MEDIUM**
    1 skein each #737 pink, #730 grenadine and #686 paddy green
- ❑ Red Heart Fine fine (fine) weight yarn (2½ oz/240 yds/ 70g per skein): **2 FINE**
    1 skein each #724 baby pink, #922 hot pink and #687 paddy green
- ❑ Sizes H/8/5mm, I/9/5.5mm, J/10/6mm and K/10½/6.5mm crochet hooks or sizes needed to obtain gauge
- ❑ Sewing needle
- ❑ Kitchen towel
- ❑ Matching sewing thread

GAUGE

Size H hook and 1 strand fine weight yarn: 2 dc rows = 1 inch
Size I hook and 1 strand medium weight yarn: 2 dc rows = 1¼ inches
Size J hook and 2 strands fine weight yarn: Rnds 1 and 2 of Front = 1½ inches across
Size K hook and 2 strands medium weight yarn: Rnds 1 and 2 of Front = 2¼ inches across

PATTERN NOTE

Join with a slip stitch unless otherwise stated.

SPECIAL STITCH

Triple treble crochet (trtr): Yo 4 times, insert hook in next st or ch sp, yo, pull lp through, [yo, pull through 2 lps on hook] 5 times.

INSTRUCTIONS

HOT PAD
FRONT

Rnd 1: With size K hook and 2 strands pink held tog as 1, ch 3, join in beg ch to form ring, ch 1, 8 sc in ring, join in beg sc. *(8 sc)*

Rnds 2 & 3: Working these rnds in **back lps** *(see Stitch Guide)*, ch 2, 2 sc in each st around, join in beg sc. Fasten off at end of last rnd. *(16 sc, 32 sc)*

Rnd 4: Working this rnd in back lps, with size K hook and 2 strands grenadine held tog as 1, join in any st, ch 4, sk next 3 sts, [sl st in next st, ch 4, sk next 3 sts] around, join in beg sl st. *(8 sc, 8 ch sps)*

Rnd 5: (Sl st, ch 4, **dtr**—*see Stitch Guide*, 3 **trtr**—*see Special Stitch*, dtr, ch 4, sl st) in each ch sp around,

join with sl st in beg sl st. Fasten off. *(8 petals)*

Rnd 6: With size I hook and 1 strand pink, working behind petals in sk st of rnd 3, join in center st of any sk 3-sc group, ch 4, [sl st in center st of next sk 3-sc group, ch 4] around, join in beg sl st. Fasten off.

Rnd 7: With size K hook and 2 strands pink held tog as 1, working in rem **front lps** *(see Stitch Guide)* of rnds 1–3, join with sl st in first st of rnd 1, [ch 3, sl st in next st] around to last st of rnd 3. Fasten off.

BACK

Rnd 1: With size I hook and 1 strand pink, ch 4, join in beg ch to form ring, ch 3 *(counts as first dc)*, 15 dc in ring, join in 3rd ch of beg ch-3. *(16 dc)*

Rnd 2: (Ch 3, dc) in first st, 2 dc in each st around, join in 3rd ch of beg ch-3. *(32 dc)*

Rnd 3: Holding Front and Back WS tog with Back facing, working in ch-4 sps of rnd 6 on Front and sts on Back at same time, ch 1, 2 sc in first st on Back and first ch-4 sp on Front, sc in next st, 2 sc in next st, sc in next st, [working in st on Back and in next ch-4 sp on Front at same time, {2 sc in next st, sc in next st} twice] around, join in beg sc. Fasten off. *(48 sc)*

Rnd 4: With size I hook and 2 strands medium weight paddy green held tog as 1, join with sc in first st, *hdc in next st, dc in each of next 2 sts, hdc in next st**, sc in each of next 2 sts, rep from * around, ending last rep at **, sc in last st, join with sl st in beg sc. *(48 sts)*

Rnd 5: Ch 1, sc in first st, *ch 2, tr in next st, 2 dtr in each of next 2 sts, tr in next st, ch 2**, sc in each of next 2 sts, rep from * around, ending last rep at **, sc in last st, join in beg sc. *(64 sts)*

Rnd 6: *Sl st in each of next 2 chs, sl st in next st, (sc, hdc) in next st, (dc, tr) in next st, ch 2, sl st in top of last tr made, (tr, dc) in next st, (hdc, sc) in next st, sl st in next st, sl st in each of next 2 chs**, sl st in each of next 2 sts, rep from * around, ending last rep at **, sl st in last st, join in joining sl st of last rnd. Fasten off.

TOWEL TOPPER
FRONT

Rnd 1: With size K hook and 2 strands baby pink held tog as 1, ch 3, join in beg ch to form ring, ch 1, 8 sc in ring, join in beg sc. *(8 sc)*

Rnds 2 & 3: Working these rnds in **back lps** *(see Stitch Guide)*, ch 2, 2 sc in each st around, join in beg sc. Fasten off at end of last rnd. *(16 sc, 32 sc)*

Rnd 4: Working this rnd in back lps, with size K hook and 2 strands hot pink held tog as 1, join in any st, ch 4, sk next 3 sts, [sl st in next st, ch 4, sk next 3 sts] around, join in beg sl st. *(8 sc, 8 ch sps)*

Rnd 5: (Sl st, ch 4, **dtr**—*see Stitch Guide*, 3 **trtr**—*see Special Stitch*, dtr, ch 4, sl st) in each ch sp around, join with sl st in beg sl st. Fasten off. *(8 petals)*

Rnd 6: With size I hook and 1 strand baby pink, working behind petals in sk sts of rnd 3, join in center st of any sk 3-sc group, ch 4, [sl st in center st of next sk 3-sc group, ch 4] around, join in beg sl st. Fasten off.

Rnd 7: With size K hook and 2 strands baby pink held tog as 1, working in rem **front lps** *(see Stitch Guide)* of rnds 1–3, join with sl st in first st of rnd 1, [ch 3, sl st in next st] around to last st of rnd 3. Fasten off.

BACK

Rnd 1: With size I hook and 1 strand baby pink, ch 4, join in beg ch to form ring, ch 3 *(counts as first dc)*, 15 dc in ring, join in 3rd ch of beg ch-3. *(16 dc)*

Rnd 2: (Ch 3, dc) in first st, 2 dc in each st around, join in 3rd ch of beg ch-3. *(32 dc)*

Rnd 3: Holding Front and Back WS tog with Back facing, working in ch-4 sps of rnd 6 on Front and sts on Back at same time, ch 1, 2 sc in first st on Back and first ch-4 sp on Front, sc in next st, 2 sc in next st, sc in next st, [working in st on Back and in next ch-4 sp on Front at same time, {2 sc in next st, sc in next st} twice] around, join in beg sc. Fasten off. *(48 sc)*

Rnd 4: With size I hook and 2 strands fine weight paddy green held tog as 1, join with sc in first st, *hdc in next st, dc in each of next 2 sts, hdc in next st**, sc in each of next 2 sts, rep from * around, ending last rep at **, sc in last st, join with sl st in beg sc. *(48 sts)*

Rnd 5: Ch 1, sc in first st, *ch 2, tr in next st, dtr in each of next 2 sts, tr in next st, ch 2**, sc in each of next 2 sts, rep from * around, ending last rep at **, sc in last st, join in beg sc. *(64 sts)*

Rnd 6: *Sl st in each of next 2 chs, sl st in next st, (sc, hdc) in next st, (dc, tr) in next st, ch 2, sl st in top of last tr made, (tr, dc) in next st, (hdc, sc) in next st, sl st in next st, sl st in each of next 2 chs**, sl st in each of next 2 sts, rep from * around, ending last rep at **, sl st in last st, join in joining sl st of last rnd. Fasten off.

FINISHING

1. Fold kitchen towel crosswise. With sewing needle and thread, st across fold; gather to fit across Back of Towel Topper and sew in place.

2. For **hanging lp**, with size G hook and fine weight paddy green, join in st on last rnd at center top, ch 12, sl st in same st. Fasten off. ❏❏

Sunflower

SKILL LEVEL

EASY

FINISHED SIZES

Hot Pad: 10½ inches across
Towel Topper: 10 inches across

MATERIALS

- ❑ Red Heart Classic medium (worsted) weight yarn (3½ oz/190 yds/ 99g per skein):
    - 1 skein each #339 mid-brown, #686 paddy green and #230 yellow
- ❑ Red Heart Fine fine (fine) weight yarn (2½ oz/240 yds/ 70g per skein):
    - 1 skein each #361 wood brown, #687 paddy green and #230 yellow
- ❑ Sizes F/5/3.75mm, G/6/4mm, H/8/5mm and I/9/5.5mm crochet hooks or sizes needed to obtain gauge
- ❑ Sewing needle
- ❑ Kitchen towel
- ❑ Matching sewing thread

GAUGE

Size F hook and 1 strand fine weight yarn: Rnds 1 and 2 of Front = 1½ inches across
Size G hook and 1 strand medium worsted weight yarn: Rnds 1 and 2 of Front = 2 inches across
Size G hook and 1 strand fine weight yarn: Rnds 1 and 2 of Back = 2½ inches across
Size H hook and 1 strand medium weight yarn: Rnds 1 and 2 of Back = 2¾ inches across
Size H hook and 2 strands fine weight yarn: 7 sts = 2 inches
Size I hook and 2 strands medium weight yarn: 3 sts = 1 inch

PATTERN NOTE

Join with a slip stitch unless otherwise stated.

SPECIAL STITCHES

Beginning popcorn (beg pc): Ch 3, 5 dc in same st, drop lp from hook, insert hook in 3rd ch of beg ch-3, pull dropped lp through.

Popcorn (pc): 6 dc in next st, drop lp from hook, insert hook in first st of 6-dc group, pull dropped lp through.

Triple treble crochet (trtr): Yo 4 times, insert hook in next st or ch sp, yo, pull lp through, [yo, pull through 2 lps on hook] 5 times.

INSTRUCTIONS

HOT PAD
FRONT

Rnd 1: With size G hook and 1 strand mid-brown, ch 5, join in beg ch to form ring, ch 1, 16 sc in ring, join in beg sc. *(16 sc)*

Rnd 2: Beg pc *(see Special Stitches)*, ch 4, sk next st, [**pc** *(see Special Stitches)* in next st, ch 4, sk next st] around, join in top of beg pc. *(8 pc, 8 ch sps)*

Rnd 3: (Sl st, beg pc) in first ch sp, ch 5, [pc in next ch sp, ch 5] around, join in top of beg pc.

Rnd 4: (Sl st, beg pc, ch 3, pc) in first ch sp, ch 3, [(pc, ch 3, pc) in next ch sp, ch 3] around, join in top of beg pc. Fasten off. *(16 pc, 16 ch sps)*

Rnd 5: With size G hook and 1 strand medium weight yellow, join with sc in any ch sp, ch 6, sk next ch sp, [sc in next ch sp, ch 6, sk next ch sp] around, join in beg sc. Fasten off. *(8 ch sps)*

Rnd 6: With size I hook and 2 strands medium weight yellow held tog as 1, join in any ch sp, (ch 3, tr, **dtr**—see Stitch Guide, **trtr**—see Special Stitches, ch 1, sl st in top of last st made, trtr, dtr, tr, ch 3, sl st) in same st, (sl st, ch 3, tr, dtr, trtr, ch 1, sl st in top of last st made, trtr, dtr, tr, ch 3, sl st) in each ch sp around, join in beg sc. Fasten off. *(8 petals)*

Rnd 7: With size G hook and 1 strand mid-brown, working behind petals in sk ch sp on rnd 4, join with sc in any sk ch sp, ch 6, [sc in next sk ch sp, ch 6] around, in beg sc. Fasten off. *(8 ch sps)*

Back

Rnd 1: With size I hook and 1 strand mid brown, ch 4, join in beg ch to form ring, ch 3 *(counts as first dc)*, 15 dc in ring, join in beg sc. *(16 dc)*

Rnd 2: (Ch 3, dc) in first st, 2 dc in each st around, join in 3rd ch of beg ch-3. *(32 dc)*

Rnd 3: Ch 3, 2 dc in next st, [dc in next st, 2 dc in next st] around, join in 3rd ch of beg ch-3. *(48 dc)*

Rnd 4: Holding Front and Back WS tog with Back facing, working in ch-6 sps on last rnd of Front and sts on Back at same time, ch 1, sc in first st on Back and in first ch sp on Front at same time, 2 sc in next st, sc in each of next 2 sts, 2 sc in next st, sc in next st, [working in next st on Back and in next ch sp on Front, sc in next st, 2 sc in next st, sc in each of next 2 sts, 2 sc in next st, sc in next st] around, join in beg sc. Fasten off. *(64 sc)*

Rnd 5: With RS facing and size H hook and 2 strands medium weight paddy green held tog as 1, join with sc in first st, *(sl st, ch 3, tr) in next st, dtr in next st, trtr in each of next 2 sts, dtr in next st, (tr, ch 3, sl st) in next st**, sc in each of next 2 sts, rep from * around, ending last rep at **, sc in last st, join in beg sc. *(8 petals)*

Rnd 6: Ch 1, sc in first st, *3 sc around next ch-3, sc in next st, (sc, dc) in next st, (dc, tr) in next st, ch 2, sl st in top of last st made, (tr, dc) in next st, (dc, sc) in next st, sc in next st, 3 sc around next ch-3**, sc in each of next 2 sts, rep from * around, ending last rep at **, sc in last st, join in beg sc. Fasten off.

TOWEL TOPPER
FRONT

Rnd 1: With size F hook and 1 strand wood brown, ch 5, join in beg ch to form ring, ch 1, 16 sc in ring, join in beg sc. *(16 sc)*

Rnd 2: Beg pc *(see Special Stitches)*, ch 4, sk next st, [**pc** *(see Special ...*

Stitches) in next st, ch 4, sk next st] around, join in top of beg pc. *(8 pc, 8 ch sps)*

Rnd 3: (Sl st, beg pc) in first ch sp, ch 5, [pc in next ch sp, ch 5] around, join in top of beg pc.

Rnd 4: (Sl st, beg pc, ch 3, pc) in first ch sp, ch 3, [(pc, ch 3, pc) in next ch sp, ch 3] around, join in top of beg pc. Fasten off. *(16 pc, 16 ch sps)*

Rnd 5: With size F hook and 1 strand fine weight yellow, join with sc in any ch sp, ch 6, sk next ch sp, [sc in next ch sp, ch 6, sk next ch sp] around, join in beg sc. Fasten off. *(8 ch sps)*

Rnd 6: With size H hook and 2 strands fine weight yellow held tog as 1, join in any ch sp, (ch 3, tr, **dtr**—*see Stitch Guide,* **trtr**—*see Special Stitches,* ch 1, sl st in top of last st made, trtr, dtr, tr, ch 3, sl st) in same st, (sl st, ch 3, tr, dtr, trtr, ch 1, sl st in top of last st made, trtr, dtr, tr, ch 3, sl st) in each ch sp around, join in beg sc. Fasten off. *(8 petals)*

Rnd 7: With size F hook and 1 strand wood brown, working behind petals in sk ch sp on rnd 4, join with sc in any sk ch sp, ch 6, [sc in next sk ch sp, ch 6] around, in beg sc. Fasten off. *(8 ch sps)*

BACK

Rnd 1: With size H hook and 1 strand wood brown, ch 4, join in beg ch to form ring, ch 3 *(counts as first dc)*, 15 dc in ring, join in beg sc. *(16 dc)*

Rnd 2: (Ch 3, dc) in first st, 2 dc in each st around, join in 3rd ch of beg ch-3. *(32 dc)*

Rnd 3: Ch 3, 2 dc in next st, [dc in next st, 2 dc in next st] around, join in 3rd ch of beg ch-3. *(48 dc)*

Rnd 4: Holding Front and Back WS tog with Back facing, working in ch-6 sps on Front and sts on Back at same time, ch 1, sc in first st on Back and in first ch sp on Front at same time, 2 sc in next st, sc in each of next 2 sts, 2 sc

in next st, sc in next st, [working in next st on Back and in next ch sp on Front, sc in next st, 2 sc in next st, sc in each of next 2 sts, 2 sc in next st, sc in next st] around, join in beg sc. Fasten off. *(64 sc)*

Rnd 5: With RS facing and size G hook and 2 strands fine weight paddy green held tog as 1, join with sc in first st, *(sl st, ch 3, tr) in next st, dtr in next st, trtr in each of next 2 sts, dtr in next st, (tr, ch 3, sl st) in next st**, sc in each of next 2 sts, rep from * around, ending last rep at **, sc in last st, join in beg sc. *(8 petals)*

Rnd 6: Ch 1, sc in first st, *3 sc around next ch-3, sc in next st, (sc, dc) in

next st, (dc, tr) in next st, ch 2, sl st in top of last st made, (tr, dc) in next st, (dc, sc) in next st, sc in next st, 3 sc around next ch-3**, sc in each of next 2 sts, rep from * around, ending last rep at **, sc in last st, join in beg sc. Fasten off.

FINISHING

1. Fold kitchen towel crosswise. With sewing needle and thread, st across fold; gather to fit across Back of Towel Topper and sew in place.

2. For **hanging lp**, with size G hook and fine weight paddy green, join in st on last rnd at center top, ch 12, sl st in same st. Fasten off. ❏❏

Anemone

FINISHED SIZES
Hot Pad: 9½ inches across
Towel Topper: 9 inches across

MATERIALS
- ❏ Red Heart Classic medium (worsted) weight yarn (3½ oz/190 yds/ 99g per skein):
  1 skein each #902 jockey red, #686 paddy green, #12 black and #1 white
- ❏ Red Heart Fine fine (fine) weight yarn (2½ oz/240 yds/ 70g per skein):
  1 skein each #904 jockey red, #687 paddy green, #12 black and #1 white
- ❏ Sizes H/8/5mm, I/9/5.5mm, J/10/6mm and K/10½/6.5mm crochet hooks or sizes needed to obtain gauge
- ❏ Sewing needle
- ❏ Kitchen towel
- ❏ Matching sewing thread

GAUGE
Size H hook and 1 strand fine weight yarn: 2 dc rows = 1 inch
Size I hook and 1 strand medium weight yarn: 2 dc rows = 1¼ inches
Size J hook and 2 strands fine weight yarn: Rnds 1 and 2 of Front = 2¾ inches across
Size K hook and 2 strands medium weight yarn: Rnds 1 and 2 of Front = 3¾ inches across

PATTERN NOTE
Join with a slip stitch unless otherwise stated.

INSTRUCTIONS
HOT PAD
FRONT
Rnd 1: With size K hook and 2 strands medium weight black held tog as 1, ch 3, join in beg ch to form ring, ch

3 (counts as first dc), 15 dc in ring, join in 3rd ch of beg ch-3. Fasten off. (16 dc)

Rnd 2: With size K hook and 2 strands medium weight white held tog as 1, join with sc in first st, sc in same st, sc in next st, [2 sc in next st, sc in next st] around, join in beg sc. Fasten off. (24 sc)

Rnd 3: With size I hook and 2 strands medium weight jockey red held tog as 1, join with sc in first st ch 1, [sc in next st, ch 1] around, join in beg sc. (24 sc, 24 ch sps)

Rnd 4: Working this rnd in **back lps** (see Stitch Guide), ch 1, sc in first st, ch 1, sk next ch sp, [sc in next st, ch 1, sk next ch sp] around, join in beg sc.

Rnd 5: Ch 1, sc in first st, *ch 1 (t dtr—see Stitch Guide) in next c sp, dtr in next st, (dtr, tr) in next c sp, ch 1**, sc in next st, rep from around, ending last rep at **, join i beg sc. Fasten off. (12 petals)

Rnd 6: With size I hook and 2 stran medium weight jockey red held to as 1, working in **front lps** (see Stitc Guide) of rnd 3, join with sc in st front of any center dtr on rnd 5, c 1, sk next ch sp, [sc in next st, ch sk next ch sp] around, join in be sc. (24 sc, 24 ch sps)

Rnd 7: Ch 1, sc in first st, *ch 1, (c tr) in next ch sp, tr in next st, (tr, c in next ch sp, ch 1**, sc in next rep from * around, ending last rep **, join. Fasten off. (12 petals)

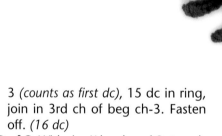

Rnd 8: With size I hook and 1 strand medium weight jockey red, working behind all petals in sk ch sps of rnd 3, join with sl st in first ch sp, ch 4, sk next ch sp, [sl st in next ch sp, ch 4, sk next ch sp] around, join in beg sl st. Fasten off. *(12 ch sps)*

BACK

Rnd 1: With size I hook and 1 strand medium weight paddy green, ch 4, join in beg ch to form ring, ch 3, 15 dc in ring, join in 3rd ch of beg ch-3. *(16 dc)*

Rnd 2: (Ch 3, dc) in first st, 2 dc in each st around, join in 3rd ch of beg ch-3. *(32 dc)*

Rnd 3: Ch 2 *(counts as first hdc)*, hdc in same st, hdc in next st, [2 hdc in next st, hdc in next st] around, join in 2nd ch of beg ch-2. *(48 hdc)*

Rnd 4: Holding Front and Back WS tog with Back facing, working in ch-4 sps on last rnd of Front and sts on Back at same time, ch 1, sc in each of first 4 sts on Back and first ch-4 sp on Front, [sc in each of next 4 sts on Back and in next ch-4 sp on Front at same time] around, join in beg sc. Fasten off. *(48 sc)*

Rnd 5: With RS facing and size I hook and 2 strands medium weight paddy green held tog as 1, join with sc in first st, *ch 9, sl st in 2nd ch from hook and in each ch across, ch 1, sl st in next st**, sc in next st, rep from * around, ending last rep at ** join in beg sc. Fasten off.

TOWEL TOPPER
FRONT

Rnd 1: With size J hook and 2 strands fine weight black held tog as 1, ch 3, join in beg ch to form ring, ch 3 *(counts as first dc)*, 15 dc in ring, join in 3rd ch of beg ch-3. Fasten off. *(16 dc)*

Rnd 2: With size J hook and 2 strands fine weight white held tog as 1, join with sc in first st, sc in same st, sc in next st, [2 sc in next st, sc in next st] around, join in beg sc. Fasten off. *(24 sc)*

Rnd 3: With size H hook and 2 strands fine weight jockey red held tog as 1, join with sc in first st ch 1, [sc in next st, ch 1] around, join in beg sc. *(24 sc, 24 ch sps)*

Rnd 4: Working this rnd in **back lps** *(see Stitch Guide)*, ch 1, sc in first st, ch 1, sk next ch sp, [sc in next st, ch 1, sk next ch sp] around, join in beg sc.

Rnd 5: Ch 1, sc in first st, *ch 1, (tr, **dtr**—*see Stitch Guide*) in next ch sp, dtr in next st, (dtr, tr) in next ch sp, ch 1**, sc in next st, rep from * around, ending last rep at **, join in beg sc. Fasten off. *(12 petals)*

Rnd 6: With size H hook and 2 strands fine weight jockey red held tog as 1, working in **front lps** *(see Stitch Guide)* of rnd 3, join with sc in st in front of any center dtr on rnd 5, ch 1, sk next ch sp, [sc in next st, ch 1, sk next ch sp] around, join in beg sc. *(24 sc, 24 ch sps)*

Rnd 7: Ch 1, sc in first st, *ch 1, (dc, tr) in next ch sp, tr in next st, (tr, dc) in next ch sp, ch 1**, sc in next st, rep from * around, ending last rep at **, join. Fasten off. *(12 petals)*

Rnd 8: With size H hook and 1 strand fine weight jockey red, working behind all petals in sk ch sps of rnd 3, join with sl st in first ch sp, ch 4, sk next ch sp, [sl st in next ch sp, ch 4, sk next ch sp] around, join in beg sl st. Fasten off. *(12 ch sps)*

BACK

Rnd 1: With size H hook and 1 strand fine weight paddy green, ch 4, join in beg ch to form ring, ch 3, 15 dc in ring, join in 3rd ch of beg ch-3. *(16 dc)*

Rnd 2: (Ch 3, dc) in first st, 2 dc in each st around, join in 3rd ch of beg ch-3. *(32 dc)*

Rnd 3: Ch 2 *(counts as first hdc)*, hdc in same st, hdc in next st, [2 hdc in next st, hdc in next st] around, join in 2nd ch of beg ch-2. *(48 hdc)*

Rnd 4: Holding Front and Back WS tog with Back facing, working in ch-4 sps on last rnd of Front and sts on Back, ch 1, sc in each of first 4 sts on Back and first ch-4 sp on Front at same time, [sc in each of next 4 sts on Back and in next ch-4 sp on Front at same time] around, join in beg sc. Fasten off. *(48 sc)*

Rnd 5: With RS facing and size H hook and 2 strands fine weight paddy green held tog as 1, join with sc in first st, *ch 9, sl st in 2nd ch from hook and in each ch across, ch 1, sl st in next st**, sc in next st, rep from * around, ending last rep at ** join in beg sc. Fasten off.

FINISHING

1. Fold kitchen towel crosswise. With sewing needle and thread, st across fold; gather to fit across Back of Towel Topper and sew in place.

2. For **hanging lp**, with size H hook and fine weight paddy green, join in st on last rnd at center top, ch 12, sl st in same st. Fasten off. ❑❑

Rose

SKILL LEVEL

EASY

FINISHED SIZES

Hot Pad: 11½ inches across
Towel Topper: 10½ inches across

MATERIALS

❑ Red Heart Classic medium (worsted) weight yarn (3½ oz/190 yds/ 99g per skein):
 1 skein each #762 claret, #686 paddy green and #230 yellow
❑ Red Heart Fine fine (fine) weight yarn (2½ oz/240 yds/ 70g per skein):
 1 skein each #918 vermilion, #687 paddy green and #230 yellow
❑ Sizes H/8/5mm, I/9/5.5mm, J/10/6mm and K/10½/6.5mm crochet hooks or sizes needed to obtain gauge
❑ Sewing needle
❑ Kitchen towel
❑ Matching sewing thread

GAUGE

Size H hook and 1 strand fine weight yarn: 2 dc rows = 1 inch
Size I hook and 1 strand medium weight yarn: 2 dc row = 1¼ inches
Size J hook and 2 strands fine weight yarn: Rnds 1–3 of Front = 3 inches across
Size K hook and 2 strands medium weight yarn: Rnds 1–3 of Front = 4 inches across

PATTERN NOTE

Join with a slip stitch unless otherwise stated.

SPECIAL STITCH

Picot: Ch 3, sl st in top of last st made.

INSTRUCTIONS
HOT PAD
FRONT

Rnd 1: With size K hook and 2 strands claret held tog as 1, ch 3, sl st in beg ch to form ring, ch 1, [sc in ring, ch 2] 8 times, join in beg sc. *(8 sc, 8 ch sps)*

Rnd 2: Sl st in first ch sp, ch 1, (sc, ch 1, 2 dc, ch 1, sc) in same sp and in each ch sp around, join in beg sc. *(8 petals)*

Rnd 3: Working behind petals, sl st around post of first sc, ch 4, [sl st around post of first sc on next petal, ch 4] around, join in beg sl st. *(8 ch sps)*

Rnd 4: Sl st in first ch sp, ch 1, (sc, ch 1, 5 dc, ch 1, sc) in same sp and in each ch sp around, join in beg sc. *(8 petals)*

Rnd 5: Working behind petals, sl st from front to back around post of first sc, ch 5, [sl st around post of first sc on next petal, ch 5] around, join in beg sl st. *(8 ch sps)*

Rnd 6: Sl st in first ch sp, ch 1, (sc, ch 1, 9 dc, ch 1, sc) in same ch sp and in each ch sp around, join in beg sc. Fasten off. *(8 petals)*

Rnd 7: With size I hook and 1 strand claret, join around post of first sc, ch 7, working behind petals, [sl st around post of first sc on next petal, ch 7] around, join in beg sl st. Fasten off.

BACK

Rnd 1: With size I hook and 1 strand claret, ch 4, join in beg ch to form ring, ch 3 *(counts as first dc)*, 15 dc in ring, join in 3rd ch of beg ch-3. *(16 dc)*

Rnd 2: (Ch 3, dc) in first st, 2 dc in each st around, join in 3rd ch of beg ch-3. *(32 dc)*

Rnd 3: Ch 3, 2 dc in next st, [dc in next st, 2 dc in next st] around, join in 3rd ch of beg ch-3. *(48 dc)*

Rnd 4: Ch 3, dc in next st, 2 dc in next st, [dc in each of next 2 sts, 2 dc in next st] around, join in 3rd ch of beg ch 3. *(64 dc)*

Rnd 5: Holding Front and Back WS tog with Back facing, working in ch-7 sps on Front and sts on Back at same time, ch 1, sc in each of first 8 sts on Back and first ch-7 sp on Front, [sc in each of next 8 sts on Back and

in next ch-7 sp on Front at same time] around, join in beg sc. Fasten off. *(64 sc)*

Rnd 6: With RS facing and size I hook and 2 strands medium weight paddy green held tog as 1, join with sc in 4th st, *hdc in next st, dc in next st, tr in next st, 2 **dtr** (see Stitch Guide) in next st, tr in next st, dc in next st, hdc in around, ending last rep at **, join in beg sc. *(72 sts)*

Rnd 7: Ch 1, sc in first st, *ch 1, dc in next st, tr in each of next 2 sts, 3 tr in next st, **picot** (see Special Stitch), 3 tr in next st, tr in each of next 2 sts, dc in next st, ch 1**, sc in next st, rep from * around, ending last rep at **, join in beg sc. Fasten off.

With tapestry needle and medium weight yellow, using **French knot** (see Fig. 1), embroider rnd 1 of Front until completely covered (see photo).

French Knot
Fig. 1

TOWEL TOPPER
FRONT

Rnd 1: With size J hook and 2 strand vermilion held tog as 1, ch 3, sl in beg ch to form ring, ch 1, [sc in ring, ch 2] 8 times, join in beg sc. *(8 sc, 8 ch sps)*

Rnd 2: Sl st in first ch sp, ch 1, (sc, ch 1, 2 dc, ch 1, sc) in same sp and in each ch sp around, join in beg sc. *(8 petals)*

Rnd 3: Working behind petals, sl st from front to back around post of first sc, ch 4, [sl st around post of first sc on next petal, ch 4] around, join in beg sl st. *(8 ch sps)*

Rnd 4: Sl st in first ch sp, ch 1, (sc, ch 1, 5 dc, ch 1, sc) in same sp and in each ch sp around, join in beg sc. *(8 petals)*

Rnd 5: Working behind petals, sl st around post of first sc, ch 5, [sl st around post of first sc on next petal, ch 5] around, join in beg sl st. *(8 ch sps)*

Rnd 6: Sl st in first ch sp, ch 1, (sc, ch 1, 9 dc, ch 1, sc) in same ch sp and in each ch sp around, join in beg sc. Fasten off. *(8 petals)*

Rnd 7: With size H hook and 1 strand vermilion, join around post of first sc, ch 7, working behind petals, [sl st around post of first sc on next petal, ch 7] around, join in beg sl st. Fasten off.

BACK

Rnd 1: With size I hook and 1 strand vermilion, ch 4, join in beg ch to form ring, ch 3 *(counts as first dc)*, 15 dc in ring, join in 3rd ch of beg ch-3. *(16 dc)*

Rnd 2: (Ch 3, dc) in first st, 2 dc in each st around, join in 3rd ch of beg ch-3. *(32 dc)*

Rnd 3: Ch 3, 2 dc in next st, [dc in next st, 2 dc in next st] around, join in 3rd ch of beg ch-3. *(48 dc)*

Rnd 4: Ch 3, dc in next st, 2 dc in next st, [dc in each of next 2 sts, 2 dc in next st] around, join in 3rd ch of beg ch 3. *(64 dc)*

Rnd 5: Holding Front and Back WS tog with Back facing, working in ch-7 sps on Front and sts on Back at same time, ch 1, sc in each of first 8 sts on Back and first ch-7 sp on Front, [sc in each of next 8 sts on Back and in next ch-7 sp on Front at same time] around, join in beg sc. Fasten off. *(64 sc)*

Rnd 6: With RS facing and size H hook and 2 strands fine weight paddy green held tog as 1, join with sc in 4th st, *hdc in next st, dc in next st, tr in next st, 2 **dtr** *(see Stitch Guide)* in next st, tr in

next st, dc in next st, hdc in next st**, sc in next st, rep from * around, ending last rep at **, join in beg sc. *(72 sts)*

Rnd 7: Ch 1, sc in first st, *ch 1, dc in next st, tr in each of next 2 sts, 3 tr in next st, **picot** *(see Special Stitch)*, 3 tr in next st, tr in each of next 2 sts, dc in next st, ch 1**, sc in next st, rep from * around, ending last rep at **, join in beg sc. Fasten off.

With tapestry needle and fine weight yellow, using **French knot** *(see fig. 1)*, embroider rnd 1 of Front until completely covered *(see photo)*.

FINISHING

1. Fold kitchen towel crosswise. With sewing needle and thread, st across fold; gather to fit across Back of Towel Topper and sew in place.

2. For **hanging lp**, with size H hook and fine weight paddy green, join in st on last rnd at center top, ch 12, sl st in same st. Fasten off. ❑❑

Zinnia

SKILL LEVEL

EASY

FINISHED SIZES
Hot Pad: 9 inches across
Towel Topper: 8 inches across

MATERIALS
❑ Red Heart Classic medium (worsted) weight yarn (3½ oz/190 yds/ 99g per skein):

4 MEDIUM

    1 skein each #584 lavender, #686 paddy green and #230 yellow
❑ Red Heart Sport (fine) weight yarn (2½ oz/240 yds/ 70g per skein):

2 FINE

    1 skein each #687 paddy green and #230 yellow
❑ TLC Baby fine (sport) weight yarn (6 oz/490 yds/170g per skein):
    1 skein #7555 lilac
❑ Sizes H/8/5mm, I/9/5.5mm, J/10/6mm and K/10½/6.5mm crochet hooks or sizes needed to obtain gauge
❑ Sewing needle
❑ Kitchen towel
❑ Matching sewing thread

GAUGE
Size H hook and 1 strand fine weight yarn: 2 dc rows = 1 inch; with 2 strands held tog, 3 sts = ¾ inch
Size I hook and 1 strand medium weight yarn: 2 dc rows = 1¼ inches; with 2 strands held tog, 3 sts = 1 inch
Size J hook and 2 strands fine weight yarn: Rnds 1–3 of Front = 2½ inches across
Size K hook and 2 strands medium weight yarn: Rnds 1–2 of Front = 3 inches across

PATTERN NOTE
Join with a slip stitch unless otherwise stated.

SPECIAL STITCHES
Beginning popcorn (beg pc): Ch 2, 5 hdc in same st, drop lp from hook, insert hook in 2nd ch of first ch-2, pull dropped lp through.
Popcorn (pc): 6 hdc in next st, drop lp from hook, insert hook in first st of 6-hdc group, pull dropped lp through.

INSTRUCTIONS
HOT PAD
FRONT
Rnd 1: With size K hook and 2 strands medium weight yellow held tog as 1, ch 5, join in beg ch to form ring, ch 1, 16 sc in ring, join in beg sc. Fasten off. *(16 sc)*

Rnd 2: With size K hook and 2 strands lavender held tog as 1, join with sl st in first st, **beg pc** *(see Special Stitches)*, ch 3, sk next st, [**pc** *(see Special Stitches)* in next st, ch 3, sk next st] around, join with sl st in beg pc. *(8 pc, 8 ch sps)*

Rnd 3: (Sl st, beg pc) in first ch sp, ch 4, [pc in next ch sp, ch 4] around, join in top of beg pc.

Rnd 4: (Sl st, beg pc, ch 3, pc) in first ch sp, ch 3, [(pc, ch 3, pc) in next ch sp, ch 3] around, join in top of beg pc. Fasten off. *(16 pc, 16 ch sps)*

Rnd 5: With size I hook and 1 strand lavender, join with sc in first ch sp, ch 8, sk next ch sp, [sc in next ch sp, ch 8, sk next ch sp] around, join in beg sc. Fasten off. *(8 ch sps)*

BACK

Rnd 1: With size I hook and 1 strand medium weight yellow, ch 4, sl st in beg ch to form ring, ch 3 *(counts as first dc)*, 15 dc in ring, join in 3rd ch of beg ch-3. Fasten off. *(16 dc)*

Rnd 2: With size I hook and 1 strand lavender, join in first st, (ch 3, dc) in same st, 2 dc in each st around, join in 3rd ch of beg ch-3. *(32 dc)*

Rnd 3: Ch 3, 2 dc in next st, [dc in next st, 2 dc in next st] around, join in 3rd ch of beg ch-3. *(48 dc)*

Rnd 4: Ch 3, dc in next st, 2 dc in next st, [dc in each of next 2 sts, 2 dc in next st] around, join in 3rd ch of beg ch-3. Fasten off. *(64 dc)*

Rnd 5: Holding Front and Back WS tog with Back facing, working in ch-8 sps on Front and sts on Back at same time, with size I hook and 1 strand medium weight paddy green, join with sc in first st on Back and in 1 ch-8 sp on Front, sc in each of next 7 sts, [sc in each of next 8 sts on Back and in next ch-8 sp on Front at same time] around, join in beg sc. Fasten off. *(64 sc)*

Rnd 6: With RS facing and size I hook and 2 strands medium weight paddy green held tog as 1, join in first st, *ch 2, dc in next st, tr in next st, **dtr** *(see Stitch Guide)* in next st, ch 1, sl st in top of last dtr made, dtr in next st, tr in next st, dc in next st, ch 2**, sl st in each of next 2 sts, rep from * around, ending last rep at **, sl st in last st, join in beg sl st. Fasten off.

TOWEL TOPPER
FRONT

Rnd 1: With size J hook and 2 strands fine weight yellow held tog as 1, ch 5, join in beg ch to form ring, ch 1, 16 sc in ring, join in beg sc. Fasten off. *(16 sc)*

Rnd 2: With size J hook and 2 strands lilac held tog as 1, join with sl st in first st, **beg pc** *(see Special Stitches)*, ch 3, sk next st, [**pc** *(see Special Stitches)* in next st, ch 3, sk next st] around, join with sl st in beg pc. *(8 pc, 8 ch sps)*

Rnd 3: (Sl st, beg pc) in first ch sp, ch 4, [pc in next ch sp, ch 4] around, join in top of beg pc.

Rnd 4: (Sl st, beg pc, ch 3, pc) in first ch sp, ch 3, [(pc, ch 3, pc) in next ch sp, ch 3] around, join in top of beg pc. Fasten off. *(16 pc, 16 ch sps)*

Rnd 5: With size H hook and 1 strand lilac, join with sc in first ch sp, ch 8, sk next ch sp, [sc in next ch sp, ch 8, sk next ch sp] around, join in beg sc. Fasten off. *(8 ch sps)*

BACK

Rnd 1: With size H hook and 1 strand fine weight yellow, ch 4, sl st in beg ch to form ring, ch 3 *(counts as first dc)*, 15 dc in ring, join in 3rd ch of beg ch-3. Fasten off. *(16 dc)*

Rnd 2: With size H hook and 1 strand lilac, join in first st, (ch 3, dc) in same st, 2 dc in each st around, join in 3rd ch of beg ch-3. *(32 dc)*

Rnd 3: Ch 3, 2 dc in next st, [dc in next st, 2 dc in next st] around, join in 3rd ch of beg ch-3. *(48 dc)*

Rnd 4: Ch 3, dc in next st, 2 dc in next st, [dc in each of next 2 sts, 2 dc in next st] around, join in 3rd ch of beg ch-3. Fasten off. *(64 dc)*

Rnd 5: Holding Front and Back WS tog with Back facing, working in ch-8 sps on Front and in sts on Back at same time, with size H hook and 1 strand fine weight paddy green, join with sc in first st on Back and in 1 ch-8 sp on Front at same time, sc in each of next 7 sts, [sc in each of next 8 sts on Back and in next ch-8 sp on Front at same time] around, join in beg sc. Fasten off. *(64 sc)*

Rnd 6: With RS facing and size H hook and 2 strands fine weight paddy green held tog as 1, join in first st, *ch 2, dc in next st, tr in next st, **dtr** *(see Stitch Guide)* in next st, ch 1, sl st in top of last dtr made, dtr in next st, tr in next st, dc in next st, ch 2**, sl st in each of next 2 sts, rep from * around, ending last rep at **, sl st in last st, join in beg sl st. Fasten off.

FINISHING

1. Fold kitchen towel crosswise. With sewing needle and thread, st across fold; gather to fit across Back of Towel Topper and sew in place.

2. For hanging lp, with size H hook and fine weight paddy green, join in st on last rnd at center top, ch 12, sl st in same st. Fasten off. ❏❏

TOLL-FREE ORDER LINE or to request a free catalog (800) LV-ANNIE (800) 582-6643
Customer Service (800) AT-ANNIE (800) 282-6643, **Fax** (800) 882-6643
Visit anniesatticcatalog.com

We have made every effort to ensure the accuracy and completeness of these instructions.
We cannot, however, be responsible for human error, typographical mistakes or variations in individual work.

ISBN: 978-1-59635-158-5

Stitch Guide

ABBREVIATIONS

beg ....begin/beginning
bpdc ....back post double crochet
bpsc .... back post single crochet
bptr ....back post treble crochet
CC ....contrasting color
ch ....chain stitch
ch- ....refers to chain or space
    previously made (i.e., ch-1 space)
ch sp ....chain space
cl .... cluster
cm ....centimeter(s)
dc ....double crochet
dec ..decrease/decreases/decreasing
dtr ....double treble crochet
fpdc ....front post double crochet
fpsc .... front post single crochet
fptr ....front post treble crochet
g ....gram(s)
hdc ....half double crochet
inc ......increase/increases/increasing
lp(s) ....loop(s)
MC .... main color
mm ....millimeter(s)
oz ....ounce(s)
pc ....popcorn
rem ....remain/remaining
rep ....repeat(s)
rnd(s) .... round(s)
RS ....right side
sc ....single crochet
sk ....skip(ped)
sl st ....slip stitch
sp(s) ....space(s)
st(s) ....stitch(es)
tog ....together
tr ....treble crochet
trtr ....triple treble
WS ....wrong side
yd(s) ....yard(s)
yo ....yarn over

Chain—ch: Yo, pull through lp on hook.

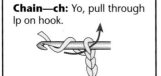

Slip stitch—sl st: Insert hook in st, yo, pull through both lps on hook.

Single crochet—sc: Insert hook in st, yo, pull through st, yo, pull through both lps on hook.

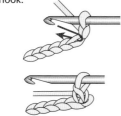

Front loop—front lp
Back loop—back lp

Front Loop   Back Loop

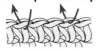

Front post stitch—fp:
Back post stitch—bp: When working post st, insert hook from right to left around post st on previous row.

Back   Front

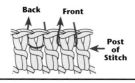

Post of Stitch

Half double crochet—hdc: Yo, insert hook in st, yo, pull through st, yo, pull through all 3 lps on hook.

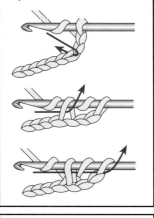

Double crochet—dc: Yo, insert hook in st, yo, pull through st, [yo, pull through 2 lps] twice.

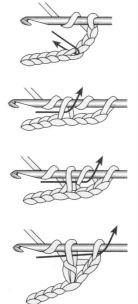

Change colors: Drop first color; with 2nd color, pull through last 2 lps of st.

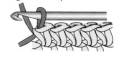

Treble crochet—tr: Yo 2 times, insert hook in st, yo, pull through st, [yo, pull through 2 lps] 3 times.

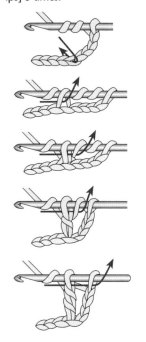

Double treble crochet—dtr: Yo 3 times, insert hook in st, yo, pull through st, [yo, pull through 2 lps] 4 times.

Single crochet decrease (sc dec): (Insert hook, yo, draw up a lp) in each of the sts indicated, yo, draw through all lps on hook.

Example of 2-sc dec

Half double crochet decrease (hdc dec): (Yo, insert hook, yo, draw lp through) in each of the sts indicated, yo, draw through all lps on hook.

Example of 2-hdc dec

Double crochet decrease (dc dec): (Yo, insert hook, yo, draw lp through, yo, draw through 2 lps on hook) in each of the sts indicated, yo, draw through all lps on hook.

Example of 2-dc dec

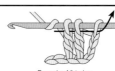

Example of 2-tr dec

Treble crochet decrease (tr dec): Holding back last lp of each st, tr in each of the sts indicated, yo, pull through all lps on hook.

US		UK
sl st (slip stitch)	=	sc (single crochet)
sc (single crochet)	=	dc (double crochet)
hdc (half double crochet)	=	htr (half treble crochet)
dc (double crochet)	=	tr (treble crochet)
tr (treble crochet)	=	dtr (double treble crochet)
dtr (double treble crochet)	=	ttr (triple treble crochet)
skip	=	miss

For more complete information, visit

AnniesAttic.com